Advanced Java Optimization Techniques

Jason Arnold

DEDICATION

I dedicate this book to my wife, Alex, who has been extremely patient with my random adventures in the wonderful land of computer science.

CONTENTS

THIS PAGE IS INTENTIONALLY LEFT BLANK

1 IDENTIFYING WHERE TO FOCUS YOUR EFFORTS

You would probably assume that a chapter on where to focus your tuning efforts would immediately start out talking about profiling. We will definitely get there, but it is not our starting point. We first need to take another step back.

Java has certainly come a long way. It has grown from an immature language with very poor performance to one of the most common development languages, with performance that rivals C/C++. Unfortunately, Java also makes it very easy for you to do things that will make it unlikely to reach these levels of performance. The goal of this book is to help you learn how to navigate the performance pitfalls of java. I cannot cover every possible pitfall or rule of thumb, but you should finish with a new methodology to employ when writing code in the future. This methodology will make it much more likely that you will write good code the first time around and you will instead be able to focus your tuning efforts on truly unique performance aspects of your code.

The first step is to realize that saying "this code isn't fast enough" is not good enough. We need to identify what types of performance issues may be occurring. In general, performance problems fall into four categories:

- Inefficient I/O
- Memory shortages
- Thread waits
- Code that requires too much CPU

Most people tend to jump write into the last category. I've intentionally made that category last, as I think it should be the last place you look.

Basic tools of the trade

Before we jump into these four categories, you should install some basic tools that you will need. This book walks you through how to analyze, tune, and test Java code running under Linux, and it assumes you have an Eclipse development environment. If your setup is different, you will be able to find similar tools for your platforms.

NMON

NMON is an excellent online and batch system monitor. In this book, I focus on using NMON as an online system monitor, but it can also be used to capture performance data from a test run, and that data can be fed into an Excel spreadsheet for analysis.

To get started with NMON, you should download it from this site: http://nmon.sourceforge.net/pmwiki.php. After you have installed NMON, you can start the online monitor simply by executing the executable that is appropriate for your distribution of Linux. This will bring up the NMON main menu where you can choose what you would like to monitor. When doing performance testing, I typically monitor processor usage (c), disk usage (d), memory usage (m), or network usage (n). This allows us to see whether code is I/O-bound or CPU-bound. We can monitor concurrency improvements by comparing cpu utilization from run to run. We can monitor disk and network throughput, which should go up as we increase the efficiency of our code.

Java Performance Analyzer

Hopefully, you are already very familiar with the process of profiling and tuning. The Java Performance Analyzer is my preferred Java profiler. You should feel free to use a different profiler if you are already comfortable with it. The Java Performance Analyzer can be downloaded from http://sourceforge.net/projects/jperfanal/. It uses HPROF to generate data on where time is being spent. This HPROF data is then fed into the tool. To generate the necessary HPROF data, you need to add the **–agentlib:hprof** argument to the JVM.

Eclipse Memory Analyzer

The Eclipse Memory Analyzer (MAT) is a plug-in for Eclipse that will take a heap dump and give you reports back on what objects are using the most memory. This can be very useful for determining where to focus your efforts on reducing your applications memory footprint. The heap dumps can easily be generated using **jmap**. You can download the Eclipse Memory Analyzer from here: https://www.eclipse.org/mat/.

I/O Inefficiency

I/O inefficiencies are typically characterized by a high disk utilization with a relatively low data transfer rate. In other words, the disk or other I/O device is doing a lot of transfers, but each of the transfers is small. Disk utilization and data transfer rates can easily be monitored using the 'm' option in NMON. Contrary to popular belief, low disk utilization rates are not usually an indication of I/O inefficiency. They are usually inefficiencies in other aspects of the application (cpu, concurrency, etc) that cause the I/O system calls to not occur as frequently as expected. If you suspect you have I/O inefficiencies, head to chapter 2 to learn how to improve your I/O performance.

High Memory Usage

High memory usage can be bad for a number of reasons. First of all, it limits the scalability of your application. If it takes x amount of RAM to run a workload of size n, it probably takes close to 2x amount of RAM to run a workload of size 2n. Reducing the value of x means that you can run larger workloads within the given RAM capacity of your machine.

Within Java, high memory usage also means higher garbage collection overhead. This is especially true if the amount of memory required by the application starts to approach the amount of memory available to the JVM. Even with concurrent garbage collectors, if the amount of free memory in the JVM gets low, the garbage collector will temporarily pause your application to free up memory. It does this to avoid OutOfMemoryErrors. These pauses can greatly impact your applications throughput and response time.

Tuning your application's memory usage means higher throughput, higher scalability, and faster response times. If you have seen OutOfMemoryErrors or you suspect your application is using more memory than it should, head to chapter 3 to learn how to tune memory usage.

Concurrency

With today's multi-core chips, the key to throughput and response time has become the efficient parallelization of code. There are many different ways to parallelize the same piece of code, and Java makes it very is for you to use inefficient parallelism. This chapter will teach you how to improve the parallelism of your code using new features in Java 5, 6, and 7. For those who want to dive right into tuning the efficiency of you code, you should start with this chapter instead of going right to chapter 5. Improving concurrency is really a subset of improving your code efficiency, and the concepts in chapter 5 will build upon the concepts in chapter 4.

Code Efficiency

In chapter 5, we will cover the remaining aspects of advanced tuning such as custom serialization, custom parsing, custom buffering, and GPU offload. I would suggest that everyone should read chapter 5, but only after reviewing the topics in the previous chapters that are applicable to your application. You can tune cpu usage efficiency all you want to, but if your code is waiting on I/O, Java monitors, or garbage collection, it's not going to do you much good!

2 IMPROVING I/O EFFICIENCY

File Channels

If you do much Java tuning and benchmarking, you will quickly realize that frequently your file I/O should be done with FileChannels. FileChannels were introduced to Java as part of NIO.

FileChannels are very simple to use. To create a FileChannel, you just call getChannel() on a RandomAccessFile. To close a FileChannel, you just call close() on it. Reading and writing with FileChannels is a little different. FileChannels leave the responsibility of buffering both input and output to the application. The key to good FileChannel performance is that you do adequately buffer both your reads and your writes. To do this you allocate a ByteBuffer object and then read or write from the ByteBuffer.

ByteBuffers can be allocated by using ByteBuffer.allocate(size) or ByteBuffer.allocateDirect(size). Direct ByteBuffers have the advantage that copying data between the ByteBuffer and the OS buffers is not needed. Primitive data is written to a ByteBuffer with the putX() methods, such as putInt(int), putDouble(double). For writing objects, you would first have to serialize to a byte[] and then write to the ByteBuffer from there. Likewise, data is read with the getX() methods. A ByteBuffer stores an internal position at all times. Data is read from or written to the current position in the ByteBuffer. The position can be queried with position() and set with position(int).

To illustrate the advantage of using FileChannels, here is a simple example that writes 1M random integers and then reads them back in. The first version is non-NIO and uses BufferedInputStream and BufferedOutputStream. The second version uses NIO and FileChannel.

```java
import java.io.BufferedInputStream;
import java.io.BufferedOutputStream;
import java.io.File;
import java.io.FileInputStream;
import java.io.FileOutputStream;
import java.nio.ByteBuffer;
import java.util.Random;


public class Example1NoNIO
{
    private static final int NUM_INTS = 1000000;
    public static void main(String[] args)
    {
        long start = System.currentTimeMillis();
        File file = new File("./test.dat");
        try
        {
            BufferedOutputStream out = new BufferedOutputStream(new
            FileOutputStream(file));
            BufferedInputStream in = new BufferedInputStream(new
            FileInputStream(file));
            Random random = new Random();
            int i = 0;
            while (i < NUM_INTS)
            {
                byte[] ba = intToBytes(random.nextInt());
                out.write(ba);
                i++;
            }

            out.close();

            i = 0;
            while (i < NUM_INTS)
            {
                byte[] ba = new byte[4];
                in.read(ba);
                int j = bytesToInt(ba);
                System.out.println(j);
                i++;
            }

            in.close();
            long end = System.currentTimeMillis();
            System.out.println("Took " + (end-start) + " milliseconds");
        }
        catch(Exception e)
        {
```

```
e.printStackTrace();
        System.exit(1);
        }
    }

    protected static int bytesToInt(byte[] val)
    {
        int ret = ByteBuffer.wrap(val).getInt();
        return ret;
    }

    protected static byte[] intToBytes(int val)
    {
        ByteBuffer bb = ByteBuffer.allocate(4);
        bb.putInt(val);
        return bb.array();
    }
}
```

Sequential read and write without NIO

```
import java.io.BufferedInputStream;
import java.io.BufferedOutputStream;
import java.io.File;
import java.io.FileInputStream;
import java.io.FileOutputStream;
import java.io.RandomAccessFile;
import java.nio.ByteBuffer;
import java.nio.channels.FileChannel;
import java.util.Random;


public class Example1NIO
{
    private static final int NUM_INTS = 1000000;
    private static final int BB_SIZE = 8000;
    public static void main(String[] args)
    {
        long start = System.currentTimeMillis();
        try
        {
            FileChannel out = new RandomAccessFile("./test.dat",
            "rws").getChannel();
            FileChannel in = new RandomAccessFile("./test.dat",
            "r").getChannel();
            Random random = new Random();
            ByteBuffer bb = ByteBuffer.allocate(BB_SIZE);
            int i = 0;
```

```
while (i < (NUM_INTS / BB_SIZE))
        {
            int j = 0;
            bb.position(0);
            while (j < (BB_SIZE / 4))
            {
                bb.putInt(random.nextInt());
                j++;
            }
            bb.position(0);
            out.write(bb);
            i++;
        }

        out.close();

        i = 0;
        while (i < (NUM_INTS / BB_SIZE))
        {
            int j = 0;
            bb.position(0);
            in.read(bb);
            bb.position(0);
            while (j < (BB_SIZE / 4))
            {
                System.out.println(bb.getInt());
                j++;
            }

            i++;
        }

        in.close();
        long end = System.currentTimeMillis();
        System.out.println("Took " + (end-start) + " milliseconds");
    }
    catch(Exception e)
    {
        e.printStackTrace();
        System.exit(1);
    }
  }
}
```

Sequential read and write with NIO

As you can see, the primary difference is that we have to handle the buffering ourselves in the NIO version. I chose to use a buffer size of 8000, which is close to the default buffer size of 8192 that the buffered streams use. On my computer, the non-NIO version took 10051ms, while the NIO version only took 2824ms. That's a 72% improvement!

Asynchronous Writes

In the NIO version of the example, we opened the output RandomAccessFile with the flag "rws", which stands for read/write/synchronous. Synchronous means that when a write method returns, the data is already on disk. You should avoid using synchronous writes whenever possible, as they decrease throughput. By replacing the "rws" in the previous example with "rw", the elapsed time drops to 2451ms. That's another 13% improvement!

Random Access

The previous examples showed sequential access. What happens if we do random access instead? To test this, I have modified the previous examples to read back the same number of integers (1M), but from random locations in the file. To modify the non-NIO example, I had to switch to using RandomAccessFile. The non-NIO version took 9931ms and the NIO version took 11631ms. This proves that using FileChannel is not always the right thing to do.

To make the comparison more apples to apples, I use the same code in both versions for writing the file. The difference between NIO and non-NIO is only in the code where we randomly read from the file. Notice that because the data access is random, we can no longer use large buffers in the NIO version. Is that the reason why NIO is less efficient here?

```java
import java.io.BufferedInputStream;
import java.io.BufferedOutputStream;
import java.io.File;
import java.io.FileInputStream;
import java.io.FileOutputStream;
import java.io.RandomAccessFile;
import java.nio.ByteBuffer;
import java.util.Random;


public class Example2NoNIO
{
    private static final int NUM_INTS = 1000000;
    public static void main(String[] args)
    {
        long start = System.currentTimeMillis();
        File file = new File("./test.dat");
        try
        {
            BufferedOutputStream out = new BufferedOutputStream(new
            FileOutputStream(file));
            RandomAccessFile in = new RandomAccessFile("./test.dat", "r");
            Random random = new Random();
            int i = 0;
            while (i < NUM_INTS)
            {
                byte[] ba = intToBytes(random.nextInt());
```

```
out.write(ba);
            i++;
        }

        out.close();

        i = 0;
        while (i < NUM_INTS)
        {
            int whichOne = Math.abs(random.nextInt()) % NUM_INTS;
            byte[] ba = new byte[4];
            in.seek(4 * whichOne);
            in.read(ba);
            int j = bytesToInt(ba);
            System.out.println(j);
            i++;
        }

        in.close();
        long end = System.currentTimeMillis();
        System.out.println("Took " + (end-start) + " milliseconds");
    }
    catch(Exception e)
    {
        e.printStackTrace();
        System.exit(1);
    }
}

protected static int bytesToInt(byte[] val)
{
    int ret = ByteBuffer.wrap(val).getInt();
    return ret;
}

protected static byte[] intToBytes(int val)
{
    ByteBuffer bb = ByteBuffer.allocate(4);
    bb.putInt(val);
    return bb.array();
}
}
```

Random read with no NIO

```
import java.io.BufferedInputStream;
import java.io.BufferedOutputStream;
import java.io.File;
import java.io.FileInputStream;
import java.io.FileOutputStream;
import java.io.RandomAccessFile;
import java.nio.ByteBuffer;
import java.nio.channels.FileChannel;
import java.util.Random;


public class Example2NIO
{
    private static final int NUM_INTS = 1000000;
    public static void main(String[] args)
    {
        long start = System.currentTimeMillis();
        File file = new File("./test.dat");
        try
        {
            BufferedOutputStream out = new BufferedOutputStream(new
FileOutputStream(file));
            FileChannel in = new RandomAccessFile("./test.dat",
"r").getChannel();
            Random random = new Random();
            int i = 0;
            while (i < NUM_INTS)
            {
                byte[] ba = intToBytes(random.nextInt());
                out.write(ba);
                i++;
            }

            out.close();

            i = 0;
            ByteBuffer bb = ByteBuffer.allocate(4);
            while (i < NUM_INTS)
            {
                int whichOne = Math.abs(random.nextInt()) % NUM_INTS;
                in.position(4 * whichOne);
                bb.position(0);
                in.read(bb);
                bb.position(0);
                int j = bb.getInt();
                System.out.println(j);
                i++;
            }
```

```
in.close();
            long end = System.currentTimeMillis();
            System.out.println("Took " + (end-start) + " milliseconds");
        }
        catch(Exception e)
        {
            e.printStackTrace();
            System.exit(1);
        }
    }

    protected static int bytesToInt(byte[] val)
    {
        int ret = ByteBuffer.wrap(val).getInt();
        return ret;
    }

    protected static byte[] intToBytes(int val)
    {
        ByteBuffer bb = ByteBuffer.allocate(4);
        bb.putInt(val);
        return bb.array();
    }
}
```

Random read with NIO

There is still one more type of read access that we frequently come across. I prefer to call it skip-sequential. Skip-sequential reading is where the starting point of the read is random, but a number of bytes are then read sequentially starting at that location. This should allow us to again have effective buffering with NIO. Let's compare non-NIO and NIO read performance for this situation. Will the larger NIO buffers put NIO performance back on top?

```java
import java.io.BufferedInputStream;
import java.io.BufferedOutputStream;
import java.io.File;
import java.io.FileInputStream;
import java.io.FileOutputStream;
import java.io.RandomAccessFile;
import java.nio.ByteBuffer;
import java.util.Random;


public class Example3NoNIO
{
    private static final int NUM_INTS = 1000000;
    private static final int NUM_TO_READ_SEQ = 128;
    public static void main(String[] args)
    {
        long start = System.currentTimeMillis();
        File file = new File("./test.dat");
        try
        {
            BufferedOutputStream out = new BufferedOutputStream(new
FileOutputStream(file));
            RandomAccessFile in = new RandomAccessFile("./test.dat", "r");
            Random random = new Random();
            int i = 0;
            while (i < NUM_INTS)
            {
                byte[] ba = intToBytes(random.nextInt());
                out.write(ba);
                i++;
            }

            out.close();

            i = 0;
            while (i < (NUM_INTS / NUM_TO_READ_SEQ))
            {
                int whichOne = Math.abs(random.nextInt()) % (NUM_INTS -
NUM_TO_READ_SEQ);
                byte[] ba = new byte[4];
                in.seek(4 * whichOne);
                int j = 0;
                while (j < NUM_TO_READ_SEQ)
                {
                    in.read(ba);
                    int k = bytesToInt(ba);
                    System.out.println(k);
                    j++;
                }
            }
```

```
i++;
        }

        in.close();
        long end = System.currentTimeMillis();
        System.out.println("Took " + (end-start) + " milliseconds");
    }
    catch(Exception e)
    {
        e.printStackTrace();
        System.exit(1);
    }
}

protected static int bytesToInt(byte[] val)
{
    int ret = ByteBuffer.wrap(val).getInt();
    return ret;
}

protected static byte[] intToBytes(int val)
{
    ByteBuffer bb = ByteBuffer.allocate(4);
    bb.putInt(val);
    return bb.array();
}
}
```

Skip sequential reading without NIO

```java
import java.io.BufferedInputStream;
import java.io.BufferedOutputStream;
import java.io.File;
import java.io.FileInputStream;
import java.io.FileOutputStream;
import java.io.RandomAccessFile;
import java.nio.ByteBuffer;
import java.nio.channels.FileChannel;
import java.util.Random;


public class Example3NIO
{
    private static final int NUM_INTS = 1000000;
    private static final int NUM_TO_READ_SEQ = 128;
    public static void main(String[] args)
    {
        long start = System.currentTimeMillis();
        File file = new File("./test.dat");
        try
        {
            BufferedOutputStream out = new BufferedOutputStream(new FileOutputStream(file));
            FileChannel in = new RandomAccessFile("./test.dat", "r").getChannel();
            Random random = new Random();
            int i = 0;
            while (i < NUM_INTS)
            {
                byte[] ba = intToBytes(random.nextInt());
                out.write(ba);
                i++;
            }

            out.close();

            i = 0;
            ByteBuffer bb = ByteBuffer.allocate(NUM_TO_READ_SEQ * 4);
            while (i < NUM_INTS / NUM_TO_READ_SEQ)
            {
                int whichOne = Math.abs(random.nextInt()) % (NUM_INTS - NUM_TO_READ_SEQ);
                in.position(4 * whichOne);
                bb.position(0);
                in.read(bb);
                bb.position(0);
                int j = 0;
                while (j < NUM_TO_READ_SEQ)
                {
```

```
int k = bb.getInt();
                    System.out.println(k);
                    j++;
                }
                i++;
            }

            in.close();
            long end = System.currentTimeMillis();
            System.out.println("Took " + (end-start) + " milliseconds");
        }
        catch(Exception e)
        {
            e.printStackTrace();
            System.exit(1);
        }
    }

    protected static int bytesToInt(byte[] val)
    {
        int ret = ByteBuffer.wrap(val).getInt();
        return ret;
    }

    protected static byte[] intToBytes(int val)
    {
        ByteBuffer bb = ByteBuffer.allocate(4);
        bb.putInt(val);
        return bb.array();
    }
}
```

Skip sequential reading with NIO

Strangely, I find that the non-NIO version completes in 8993ms on my machine, but that the NIO version takes 9764ms. What's going on? Profiling shows me what the problem is. It turns out that calling position(long) on a FileChannel object is a very slow operation. All of the random positioning outweighs the benefits of NIO. As NUM_TO_READ_SEQ increases, and the number of calls to position() decreases, NIO will eventually outperform non-NIO.

To summarize this section, NIO offers major performance advantages for sequential reads. RandomAccessFile frequently, but not always, outperforms NIO for random access.

Compressed Socket I/O

Next, let's take a look at improving socket I/O performance. You should already be using buffered input and output streams for your socket I/O. Remember, buffering is always a good thing except for some random access scenarios. With network I/O, there is no such thing as random access, so always make sure you are using buffering!

What else could possibly be done to improve performance? As you scale your application, eventually you will saturate one or more of you network links. At this point, your application will not continue to scale. What if the network traffic could be compressed so that more data could fit on the link? It is perfectly possible to do compressed network I/O in Java. Unfortunately, most of the methods that are documented require major application changes and are very finicky and error prone. This is because most documented methods try to do compression at the stream level. In this section, I will show you how to do compression at the socket level instead. By doing network compression in this manner, it is transparent to the code that is doing the I/O.

On the server side we are going to replace all of our ServerSockets with CompressedServerSockets. The code for CompressedServerSocket is very simple and is shown below.

```java
import java.io.IOException;
import java.net.ServerSocket;
import java.net.Socket;

public final class CompressedServerSocket extends ServerSocket {

  /**
   * Creates a compressed server socket.
   *
   * @param port the port number, or <code>0</code> to use any free port.
   * @throws java.io.IOException
   */
  public CompressedServerSocket(int port) throws IOException {
    super(port);
  }

  @Override
  public Socket accept() throws IOException {
    Socket socket = new CompressedSocket();
    implAccept(socket);
    return socket;
  }
}
```
Compressed server-side socket

CompressedServerSocket in turn relies on CompressedSocket. All regular Sockets should also get replaced with CompressedSockets. The code for CompressedSocket is also very simple. We only need to override the getInputStream() and getOutputStream() methods from Socket. We also update the close() method to close our custom input and output streams.

```java
import java.io.IOException;
import java.io.InputStream;
import java.io.OutputStream;
import java.net.Socket;

public final class CompressedSocket extends Socket {

  private CompressedOutputStream out;
  private CompressedInputStream in;


  /**
   * Creates a compressed stream socket and connects it to the specified
port
   * number on the named host.
   *
   * @param host the host name, or <code>null</code> for the loopback
address.
   * @param port the port number.
   * @exception  IOException  if an I/O error occurs when creating the
socket.
   * @see Socket#Socket(java.lang.String, int)
   */
  public CompressedSocket(String host, int port) throws IOException {
    super(host, port);
  }


  /**
   * Creates an unconnected socket, with the
   * system-default type of SocketImpl.
   *
   * @see Socket#Socket()
   */
  public CompressedSocket() {
    super();
  }



  @Override
  public InputStream getInputStream() throws IOException {
    if (in == null) {
      in = new CompressedInputStream(super.getInputStream());
    }
    return in;
  }
```

```java
@Override
  public OutputStream getOutputStream() throws IOException {
    if (out == null) {
      // buffer should be as large as possible!
      out = new CompressedOutputStream(super.getOutputStream());
    }
    return out;
  }

  @Override
  public void close() throws IOException {
    if (out != null) {
      out.close();
      out = null;
    }
    if (in != null) {
      in.close();
      in = null;
    }
    /**
     * notice that super.close() may invoke out.close() and in.close()
 again
     * depending on the implementation of SocketImpl in Socket.
     * However, the CompressedIn/OutputStream can deal with that.
     */
    super.close();
  }

}
```

Socket that uses input and output compression

CompressedSocket in turn relies on CompressedInputStream and CompressedOutputStream. This is where the real work happens. The data is compressed using the Java Deflater class. The purpose of this book is not to teach the Java compression API, so don't get too hung up if you can't understand all of the code.

```java
import java.io.FilterOutputStream;
import java.io.IOException;
import java.io.OutputStream;
import java.util.zip.Deflater;

/**
 * Stream to write compressed data to the underlying output stream.
 * <p>
 * Replacement for GZIPOutputStream and ZipOutputStream of java.util.zip
 * capable for communication link streams like tcp-sockets.
 * The standard classes are only file-capable (relying on EOF-detection).
 * In comlinks, however, there are several packets instead of a single
file.
 * Hence, the stream must be blocked, i.e. the (varying) blocksize must
 * become part of the protocol to allow the corresponding input stream
 * to detect the end of the packets.
 * Furthermore, we optimize to compress only packets larger than a certain
size.
 * All smaller packets will be transferred uncompressed.
 * For the packet size we use the first two bytes in the packet (short),
while
 * MSBit signals whether the packet is compressed or not.
 * Because of this, the maximum buffer size is limited to 32K - 1.
 */
public final class CompressedOutputStream extends FilterOutputStream {

  /**
   * The maximum compression buffer size. The larger the buffer, the
better the compression.
   */
  public static final int MAX_BUFFER_SIZE = Short.MAX_VALUE;


  final static int COMPRESSED = MAX_BUFFER_SIZE + 1;     // 0x8000 MSBit: 1
= compressed, 0 = uncompressed

  private int minCompressSize;          // minimum packet size for
compression
  private int bufSize;                  // buffer size

  private byte[] orgBuf;                // original uncompressed data
buffer
  private int orgLen;                   // number of bytes in orgBuf
  private Deflater deflater;            // the zip deflater
  private byte[] defBuf;                // deflated/compressed output data
buffer
  private int defLen;                   // number of bytes in defBuf
  private byte[] byteBuf = new byte[1]; // single byte buffer for write(b)
  private boolean closed;               // true if closed
```

```
  // for statistic only (Level.FINE must be enabled)
  private long totalWritten;            // total number of bytes written
by application
  private long totalCompressed;         // number of compressed bytes
written to stream
  private long totalUncompressed;       // number of uncompressed bytes
written to stream

  /**
   * Creates a compressed output stream.
   *
   * @param out the underlying output stream (e.g. from a socket)
   * @param bufSize the buffer size for compression. Packets larger than
bufSize are split.
   * @param minCompressSize the minimum compressed packet size. Smaller
packets pass the stream uncompressed.
   */
  public CompressedOutputStream(OutputStream out, int bufSize, int
minCompressSize) {

    super(out);

    if (bufSize <= minCompressSize || bufSize > MAX_BUFFER_SIZE) {
      throw new IllegalArgumentException("illegal bufSize [" +
minCompressSize + " < ?" + bufSize + "? <= " + MAX_BUFFER_SIZE + "]");
    }

    this.bufSize         = bufSize;
    this.minCompressSize = minCompressSize;

    orgBuf         = new byte[bufSize];
    deflater       = new Deflater(Deflater.BEST_COMPRESSION, true);  //
with noWrap: less metadata -> better compression
    defBuf         = new byte[bufSize];
  }

  /**
   * Creates a compressed output stream with maximum allowed buffersize
(32K-1) and
   * a default minCompressSize of 64.
   *
   * @param out the underlying output stream
   */
  public CompressedOutputStream(OutputStream out) {
    this(out, MAX_BUFFER_SIZE, 64);
  }
```

```
/**
 * Writes the specified <code>byte</code> to this output stream.
 *
 * @param      b    the <code>byte</code>.
 * @exception  IOException  if an I/O error occurs.
 */
@Override
public void write(int b) throws IOException {
  byteBuf[0] = (byte)b;
  write(byteBuf, 0, 1);
}


/**
 * Writes <code>len</code> bytes from the specified
 * <code>byte</code> array starting at offset <code>off</code> to
 * this output stream.
 * <p>
 * Packets larger than the buffer size will be split and written to
 * the underlying output stream as separate packets.
 *
 * @param      b      the data.
 * @param      off    the start offset in the data.
 * @param      len    the number of bytes to write.
 * @exception  IOException  if an I/O error occurs.
 */
@Override
public void write(byte[] b, int off, int len) throws IOException {

  totalWritten += len;

  while (len > 0) {

    int num = len;
    if (num > bufSize - orgLen) {
      num = bufSize - orgLen;    // align to buffersize
    }

    System.arraycopy(b, off, orgBuf, orgLen, num);
    off    += num;
    len    -= num;
    orgLen += num;

    if (orgLen >= bufSize) {
      // buffer full: write/compress it!
      flushBuffer();
    }
  }
```

```
  }


  /**
   * Flushes this output stream and forces any buffered output bytes
   * to be written out to the stream.
   *
   * @exception  IOException  if an I/O error occurs.
   */
  @Override
  public void flush() throws IOException {
    flushBuffer();     // write any pending data
    super.flush();
  }


  /**
   * Overridden to print stats only
   */
  @Override
  public void close() throws IOException {
    if (!closed) {
      closed = true;
      super.close();
    }
  }


  /**
   * @return true if closed
   */
  public boolean isClosed() {
    return closed;
  }


  /**
   * Writes the header.
   *
   * @param size the logical packet size
   * @param compressed is true if packet is compressed, false if
uncompressed
   */
  private void writeHeader(int size, boolean compressed) throws
IOException {
    if (compressed) {
      size |= COMPRESSED;
    }
```

```java
    // msb first
    out.write((size >>> 8) & 0xff);
    out.write(size & 0xff);
  }



  /**
   * Flushes the buffer.
   * If the packet size is large enough, the data will be compressed.
   * If the compressed data is smaller than the original data, a
compressed
   * packet will be written. Otherwise, an uncompressed packet is written
   * to the underlying output stream.
   */
  private void flushBuffer() throws IOException {
    if (orgLen > 0) {
      if (orgLen >= minCompressSize) {
        // compress the data
        deflater.reset();    // sadly we must reset() cause of finish() :(
        deflater.setInput(orgBuf, 0, orgLen);
        deflater.finish();
        defLen = 0;
        while (!deflater.finished()) {
          int num = deflater.deflate(defBuf, defLen, bufSize - defLen);
          if (num <= 0) {
            // can this really happen? Yes: if minCompressSize is too
small!
            if (deflater.needsInput()) {
              throw new IOException("Deflater needs more input! Bytes in
buffer: " + orgLen);
            }
          }
          defLen += num;
        }
        if (defLen < orgLen) {
          // deflate
          writeHeader(defLen, true);
          out.write(defBuf, 0, defLen);
          totalCompressed += defLen;
          orgLen = 0;
          return;
        }
      }

      // uncompressed packet
      writeHeader(orgLen, false);
      out.write(orgBuf, 0, orgLen);
      totalUncompressed += orgLen;
```

```
      orgLen = 0;
    }
  }
}
```

Compressed output stream for CompressedSocket

The input side is very similar, but we instead use the Java Inflater class to decompress the compressed data.

```java
import java.io.EOFException;
import java.io.FilterInputStream;
import java.io.IOException;
import java.io.InputStream;
import java.util.zip.DataFormatException;
import java.util.zip.Inflater;

/**
 * Stream to read compressed data from the underlying input stream.<br>
 *
 * Counterpart to CompressedOutputStream.
 */
public final class CompressedInputStream extends FilterInputStream {

  private byte[] infBuf;                 // buffer holding compressed data
for the inflater (size is dynamically adapted)
  private Inflater inflater;             // zip inflater
  private boolean compressed;            // true if current packet is
compressed and inf... is valid
  private int readPending;               // number of bytes pending to read
from underlying stream
  private byte[] byteBuf;                // single byte buffer for read()
  private boolean closed;                // true if closed

  // for statistic only (Level.FINE must be enabled)
  private long totalRead;                // total number of bytes read by
application
  private long totalCompressed;          // number of compressed bytes read
from stream
  private long totalUncompressed;        // number of uncompressed bytes
read from stream



  /**
   * Creates a new compressed input stream.<br>
   *
   * The buffersize adapts dynamically to the packet size.
   *
```

```
  * @param in the underlying input stream
  */
 public CompressedInputStream(InputStream in) {
   super(in);
   inflater = new Inflater(true);
   byteBuf = new byte[1];
 }


 @Override
 public void close() throws IOException {
   if (!closed) {
     closed = true;
     super.close();
   }
 }


 /**
  * Returns the closed state.
  *
  * @return true if closed
  */
 public boolean isClosed() {
   return closed;
 }


 /**
  * Reads the next uncompressed byte of data from the input stream.
  *
  * @return     the next byte of data, or <code>-1</code> if the end of
the
  *             stream is reached.
  * @exception IOException  if an I/O error occurs.
  */
 @Override
 public int read() throws IOException {
   int num = read(byteBuf, 0, 1);
   return num < 0 ? num : byteBuf[0];
 }


 /**
  * Reads up to <code>len</code> uncompressed bytes of data from this
input stream
  * into an array of bytes.
  *
```

```
 * @param       b       the buffer into which the data is read.
 * @param       off     the start offset in the destination array
<code>b</code>
 * @param       len     the maximum number of bytes read.
 * @return      the total number of bytes read into the buffer, or
 *              <code>-1</code> if there is no more data because the end
of
 *              the stream has been reached.
 *
 * @exception  IOException  if an I/O error occurs.
 */
@Override
public int read(byte[] b, int off, int len) throws IOException {

    // bounds check
    if (len <= 0 || off < 0 || off + len > b.length) {
        if (len == 0) {
            // reading 0 bytes is explicitly allowed and tolerates illegal
values of b and off
            return 0;        // see SocketInputStream
        }
        throw new ArrayIndexOutOfBoundsException("b.length=" + b.length + ",
off=" + off + ", len=" + len);
    }

    int count = 0;      // number of bytes read

    while (count == 0) {
        if (compressed) {
            // get decompressed data from inflater
            try {
                count = inflater.inflate(b, off, len);
            }
            catch (DataFormatException e) {
                throw new IOException("decompression failed", e);
            }

            if (count <= 0) {    // is <0 shouldn't be possible, but...
                // all data from infBuf has been decompressed
                if (readPending == 0) {
                    // read header of next packet
                    if (readHeader() == false) {
                        return -1;     // end of stream reached
                    }
                    if (!compressed) {
                        // new packet is not compressed: start over
                        continue;
                    }
```

```
        }
        if (inflater.needsInput()) {
          // read as much as you can into the buffer.
          // At best: read the whole packet.
          int num = in.read(infBuf, 0, readPending);
          if (num < 0) {
            // unexpected EOF
            throw new EOFException();
          }
          readPending -= num;
          totalCompressed += num;
          // pass compressed data to the inflater
          inflater.setInput(infBuf, 0, num);
        }
        else {
          throw new IOException("nothing decompressed but inflator does
not request more input");
        }
      }
    }
    else {
      // uncompressed
      if (readPending == 0) {
        // read header of next packet
        if (readHeader() == false) {
          return -1;
        }
        if (compressed) {
          // next packet is compressed: start over
          continue;
        }
      }
      // read directly bypassing the buffer
      count = readPending;
      if (count > len)  {
        count = len;    // align to max. requested len
      }
      count = in.read(b, off, count);

      if (count < 0) {
        throw new EOFException();
      }
      readPending -= count;
      totalUncompressed += count;
    }
  }

  totalRead += count:
```

```
      return count;
  }



  /**
   * Reads the header of the next packet.
   *
   * @return true if next packet loaded, false if end of stream
   */
  private boolean readHeader() throws IOException {

    // read header first
    int ch1 = in.read();
    if (ch1 < 0) {
      return false;    // EOF
    }
    int ch2 = in.read();
    if (ch2 < 0) {
      throw new EOFException();
    }

    readPending = (ch1 << 8) + (ch2 << 0);
    compressed = ((readPending & CompressedOutputStream.COMPRESSED) ==
CompressedOutputStream.COMPRESSED);
    readPending &= ~CompressedOutputStream.COMPRESSED;

    if (compressed) {
      // reset decompressor on each new compressed packet
      inflater.reset();
      // make sure buffer is large enough to hold the whole packet.
      if (infBuf == null || infBuf.length < readPending) {
        // allocate larger buffer
        infBuf = new byte[readPending];
      }
    }

    return true;
  }

}
```

Compressed input stream for CompressedSocket

With these 4 classes, your application code can continue to do I/O just as it did before, but now you won't be taking up as much bandwidth on your network links. I have frequently seen my application scale another 2x after implementing CompressedSocket with minimal response time impact!

3 REDUCING MEMORY USAGE

Memory Monitoring

Before we get started on how to reduce memory usage, we need to talk about how to monitor memory usage. You need to see how your application is using memory before you can determine that you have a problem or attempt to fix it. The easiest way to monitor the memory usage of your application is to run a thread that periodically wakes up, checks to see how much memory is free, prints a message to stdout, stderr, or a file, and goes back to sleep. I prefer to print to stdout or stderr so I can see in real time how free memory is changing, but the choice is up to you.

Below I present a ResourceMonitor class that performs the actions listed above.

```java
public final class ResourceMonitor extends Thread
{
    protected static final int SLEEP_TIME = 10000;
    protected static final long maxMemory;

    static
    {
        maxMemory = Runtime.getRuntime().maxMemory();
    }

    public void run()
    {
        while (true)
        {
            System.out.println(((Runtime.getRuntime().freeMemory() +
maxMemory - Runtime.getRuntime().totalMemory()) * 100.0) / (maxMemory *
1.0) + "% free");
            try
            {
                Thread.sleep(SLEEP_TIME);
```

```
            }
            catch(Exception e) {}
        }
    }
}
```

Class for monitoring memory usage

Which Objects Are Using The Memory?

If ResourceMonitor shows you that your application is using too much memory, the next step is to determine what objects are using all that memory. For small to moderate heap sizes, this is best done using the Memory Analyzer Tool (MAT). See chapter 1 for how to download MAT. To use MAT, you need to generate a heap dump at a time where the application has run the JVM low on memory. To do this, run your application and monitor the output from ResourceMonitor. When you see that your application has run the JVM low on memory use the jmap command to generate a heap dump. This heap dump then needs to be transferred to your workstation and opened in MAT in Eclipse. MAT will generate reports showing how much memory each type of object is using.

If your heap size is large, MAT will take too long to process the heap dump. In these cases, use the jmap –histo command to generate a report that shows how much space each type of object is using. This approach is very fast, even for large heaps.

Garbage Collection Issues

Even if your application isn't running the JVM out of memory, it may still experience long garbage collection pauses. In these scenarios, your best approach is to limit the number of new object allocations as much as possible. For example, rather than allocating new HashMaps over and over, just clear() a HashMap that you are done with and reuse it. Object reuse can go a long ways towards reducing garbage collection pauses.

If this is not enough to solve your problem, you should be aware that there is a commercial grade JVM on the market that has much better garbage collection performance with almost no application pauses. I have used it in several of my applications where garbage collection pauses were a problem. The JVM is from a company called Azul and the product is called Zing. You can get more information at http://www.azulsystems.com/technology/c4-garbage-collector. While Zing is, in general, not free, they do offer it for free for open source projects. You can find more info here: http://www.azulsystems.com/press/azul-systems-announces-new-initiative-to-support-open-source-community-with-free-zing-jvm.

Reducing Object Memory Usage

Most of the time you will find that it is Strings, Java Collections classes, or wrapper types that are using the majority of your memory. If you see that it is wrapper types (Integer, Long, Double, etc) you should try to replace these with primitive types if at all possible. The primitive types will use 50+% less memory than the corresponding wrapper type.

Unfortunately, one of the most common uses of the wrapper classes is with Java collections, and it is not possible to use primitive types with collections. However, there are several solutions to this problem. If you are using a List, you may want to consider using an array instead, since arrays allow primitive types. You can also go to the GrepCode website, pull down a copy of the Java source for the collection class in question, and modify it to use whatever primitive type you need. This is frequently the solution with the fastest performance (other than using an array). This is an insight that you will see over and over throughout this book. Frequently you can improve your application quite a bit by using custom versions of the Java internal classes. The classes that come with Java are designed to be general-purpose. They are not tuned for your applications needs. This approach can make your code harder to read and it can be time-consuming, but I have achieved over 50% performance improvement just by using custom versions of Java internal classes.

If you need to reduce memory usage, but response time and throughput aren't as important to you, you may want to consider using Trove. Trove offers a large number of drop-in replacements for collections classes which allow primitive data types. You can find more information on Trove at http://trove.starlight-systems.com/.

Strings take up a surprising amount of space in Java. You might suspect that a String would contain a 4 byte length and a byte[] containing the character data. You would be very wrong. The actual size of a String object depends on the JVM, but at a minimum you can expect 38 bytes plus 2 bytes for every character in the String. The reason for 2 bytes per character is that a String is backed with a char[] and in Java a char is 16 bits, versus 8 bits in C/C++.

So what can be done to reduce the amount of memory used by Strings? Fortunately, most applications that have a large number of Strings have numerous String objects which all contain the same string. In these cases, you can force the JVM to use the same String object for all Strings that have the same string value. To do this, you must call the intern() method on every new String that you allocate. The intern method() stores the String object in a lookup table if the lookup table did not already contain an equal String. If the lookup table contains an equal String, a reference to that String is returned instead of the original object.

Only try this approach with Java 7 or later. In Java 6, the lookup table was stored in the garbage collector's permanent generation. Since the size of the permanent generation is fixed at JVM startup, it can be extremely painful to size it correctly for interning. In Java 7, the lookup table has been moved to the normal heap. Of course, you could always trying to build your own string interning method in Java 6, but my experience has shown that the Java internal interning performs much better than anything you can write.

Disk Backed Collection Classes

In some of my applications, I have a need to use collections classes that are so large they couldn't possibly fit in the heap, even after applying the recommendations above. In these situations, I use a set of disk backed collections classes that I have built.

The basic idea is simple. A disk backed collection contains a regular Java collection class. Under normal conditions, new objects that are being added to the collection get added to this normal in memory Java collection. If free memory becomes low, new objects being added are instead directed to disk. Additionally, a "cleaner thread" is started that moves existing data from the in-memory Java collection to disk. If the amount of free memory goes back up and crosses a high threshold (versus the low threshold that triggers the cleaner thread), an "import thread" is started which moves data from disk back into memory. The get() method of the collection has been updated to first check the in-memory collection and then check disk. As long as the cleaner and import threads are written correctly, there is no need for synchronization between gets() or puts() and the cleaner/import threads. The only synchronization that is needed is to make sure that no cleaner or import thread is running when existing data gets updated. If data in the collection is being replaced or deleted, a read lock of a ReentrantReadWriteLock is obtained. Since the cleaner and import threads acquire a write lock of the same ReentrantReadWriteLock, we can assure that no cleaner or import thread is running during the data modification operations. The code of such a class is much too complex for me to include in this book, so let me give you some further suggestions so that you can create such a class for yourself.

For starters, you need to have a means of tracking whether the JVM is in a low memory state, where free memory is lower than some low threshold, or if the JVM is in a high free memory state, where free memory is higher than some high threshold. You want to make sure there is enough separation between these two thresholds so that you don't thrash between transferring data from memory to disk and transferring it back from disk to memory. The ResourceMonitor class that was shown previously in this chapter gives you everything you need to monitor current free memory conditions. You also need a fast efficient way to store data on disk. Personally, I would recommend always appending to the end of a file and not dealing with trying to reclaim free space. I would also recommend using custom serialization, as discussed in the final chapter of this book, instead of standard Java serialization. You will be amazed by the performance difference.

The last thing that you need is a fast way to determine if the desired value is on disk, and if so where it is on disk. I take care of this by keeping an in-memory ConcurrentHashMap which maps the key or index of the data to find to an offset in the file where the data is stored.

One final thing worth pointing out is that I frequently write the code such that data can be spread across multiple physical disks for higher read/write throughput.

4 GETTING BETTER CONCURRENCY

Building Your Own Profiler

Most people profile their application using some profiling tool, such as the Java Performance Analyzer that I mentioned in chapter 1. Most profiling tools work by using HPROF output as their input. I highly recommend that you use this approach. However, I also recommend that you build your own profiler into your application. I have seen many times where the Java Performance Analyzer shows me some hot spots, but that doing my own profiling shows me others. Doing your own profiling seems to be much better at pointing out synchronization contention. It will point out the exact synchronized blocks that are causing a lot of wait time.

It's not hard at all to build your own profiler and stick it into your code. Java gives you all the methods you need to grab all the currently running threads and determine what method they are in and what line number they are on. From there, you can easily keep track of which line numbers the most time is being spent in. I typically implement my profiler as an extension to the ResourceMonitor class that I presented in the previous chapter. If you did not read that chapter, you may want to go back and just read that section. I then use a final boolean flag that enables or disables profiling. Code for the updated ResourceMonitor is shown below

```
import java.io.File;
import java.io.PrintWriter;
import java.util.HashMap;
import java.util.Map;
import java.util.TreeSet;

public final class ResourceMonitorWithProfiler extends Thread
{
    protected static final int SLEEP_TIME = 10000;
    protected static final long maxMemory;
    protected static final boolean PROFILE = true;

    static
    {
        maxMemory = Runtime.getRuntime().maxMemory();
    }

    public void run()
    {
        if (PROFILE)
        {
            new ProfileThread().start();
        }

        while (true)
        {
            System.out.println(((Runtime.getRuntime().freeMemory() +
maxMemory - Runtime.getRuntime().totalMemory()) * 100.0) / (maxMemory *
1.0) + "% free");
            try
            {
                Thread.sleep(SLEEP_TIME);
            }
            catch(Exception e) {}
        }
    }

    private static final class ProfileThread extends Thread
    {
        protected HashMap<CodePosition, CodePosition> counts = new
HashMap<CodePosition, CodePosition>();
        long samples = 0;

        private static final class CodePosition implements Comparable
        {
            String file;
            String method;
            int lineNum;
            long count = 0;
```

```java
        public CodePosition(String file, int lineNum, String method)
        {
            this.file = file;
            this.lineNum = lineNum;
            this.method = method;
        }

        public boolean equals(Object rhs)
        {
            CodePosition r = (CodePosition)rhs;
            if (file.equals(r.file) && lineNum == r.lineNum)
            {
                return true;
            }

            return false;
        }

        public int hashCode()
        {
            return file.hashCode() + lineNum;
        }

        public int compareTo(Object rhs)
        {
            CodePosition cp = (CodePosition)rhs;
            if (count < cp.count)
            {
                return 1;
            }

            if (count > cp.count)
            {
                return -1;
            }

            return 0;
        }
    }

    public void run()
    {
        while (true)
        {
            Map<Thread, StackTraceElement[]> map =
Thread.getAllStackTraces();
            for (Map.Entry entry : map.entrySet())
            {
```

```
                        StackTraceElement[] trace =
(StackTraceElement[])entry.getValue();

                        int i = 0;
                        while (i < trace.length)
                        {
                            String file = trace[i].getClassName();
                            int lineNum = trace[i].getLineNumber();
                            String method = trace[i].getMethodName();
                            CodePosition cp = new CodePosition(file, lineNum,
method);

                            CodePosition cp2 = counts.get(cp);
                            if (cp2 == null)
                            {
                                cp.count++;
                                counts.put(cp, cp);
                            }
                            else
                            {
                                cp2.count++;
                            }

                            i++;
                        }
                }

                samples++;

                TreeSet<CodePosition> set = new TreeSet<CodePosition>();
                for (CodePosition cp : counts.values())
                {
                    if (cp.count * 100 / samples >= 1)
                    {
                        set.add(cp);
                    }
                }
                try
                {
                    PrintWriter out = new PrintWriter(new
File("./profile.new"));
                    for (CodePosition cp : set)
                    {
                        out.println(cp.file + "." + cp.method + ":" +
cp.lineNum + " " + (cp.count * 100 / samples) + "%");
                    }
                    out.close();
                    new File("./profile.new").renameTo(new
File("./profile.txt"));
                }
```

```
catch(Exception e)
            {
                    e.printStackTrace();
                    System.exit(1);
            }
        }
    }
  }
}
```

Building your own profiler

Avoiding Synchronization

Assume that profiling shows you some synchronized blocks that are hot spots. What could you do to improve them? Let's use some examples to illustrate some Java constructs that allow you to avoid or minimize synchronization. We will improve the example and look at the performance along the way.

We need an algorithm that is simple, easy to parallelize, and will demonstrate the objectives of this chapter. For this I have chosen a simple algorithm that can be used to calculate pi. It turns out that the following formula can be used to calculate pi.

$$\pi = \int_0^1 \frac{16y - 16}{y^4 - 2y^3 + 4y - 4} \, dy.$$

Don't be scared if you don't remember your calculus. The formula just says that the area bounded by x=0, x=1, y=0, and y = ((16y–16) / (y^4-2y^3+4y-4)) is equal to pi. Parts above the x-axis count as positive. Parts below the x-axis count as negative. Let's start with a naïve implementation that will use this formula to calculate pi.

```
public class PiFullSynced
{
    private static final int NUM_THREADS = 8;
    private static final double step = 0.125 * (1.0 / (4.0 * 1024.0 *
1024.0)); //will use 2^25 steps to calculate pi
    private static double pi = 0;
    public static void main(String[] args)
    {
        long start = System.currentTimeMillis();
        int i = 0;
        IntegrationThread[] threads = new IntegrationThread[NUM_THREADS];
        while (i < NUM_THREADS)
        {
            threads[i] = new IntegrationThread(i * 0.125, (i+1) * 0.125);
//integrate from start to end
            threads[i].start();
            i++;
        }

        i = 0;
```

```java
        while (i < NUM_THREADS)
        {
            while (true)
            {
                try
                {
                    threads[i].join();
                    break;
                }
                catch(InterruptedException e)
                {
                    continue;
                }
            }
            i++;
        }

        System.out.println("Pi is approximately " + pi);
        long end = System.currentTimeMillis();
        System.out.println("Execution took " + (end-start) + "ms");
    }

    private static final class IntegrationThread extends Thread
    {
        private double start;
        private double end;

        public IntegrationThread(double start, double end)
        {
            this.start = start;
            this.end = end;
        }

        public void run()
        {
            while (start < end)
            {
                double temp = ((16.0 * start - 16.0) / (Math.pow(start, 4)
                - 2 * Math.pow(start, 3) + 4 * start - 4)) * step;
                synchronized(PiFullSynced.class)
                {
                    pi += temp;
                }

                start += step;
            }
        }
    }
}
```

In this naïve example, we update the global pi variable after computing each step. Since the pi variable is static, we synchronize on PiFullySynced.class every time we update its value. On my 8 core machine, this version takes 11474ms to complete. That's not too good.

Some of you may be saying "but that's a really dumb way to write that code". You would be correct. But, it's a simple example designed to illustrate a couple points that can be applied to any real-world programming problem. It tends to be very obvious when the programming problem at hand is very simple, but for someone reason we tend to revert to full synchronization when the problem becomes more complex

What happens if we take out the synchronization and instead use a global AtomicDouble. Wait! Java offers AtomicLong, AtomicInt, and AtomicBoolean, but no AtomicDouble! However, Java provides us with an AtomicReference class, which is all we need to write our own AtomicDouble class. The AtomicDouble class is listed below.

```java
import java.util.Comparator;
import java.util.concurrent.atomic.AtomicReference;

public final class AtomicDouble extends Number implements
Comparable<AtomicDouble> {
    protected static final long serialVersionUID = -2419445336101038676L;
    protected AtomicReference<Double> value;

    // Constructors
    public AtomicDouble() {
        this(0.0);
    }

    public AtomicDouble(double initVal) {
        this(new Double(initVal));
    }

    public AtomicDouble(Double initVal) {
        value = new AtomicReference<Double>(initVal);
    }

    public AtomicDouble(AtomicDouble initVal) {
        this(initVal.getDoubleValue());
    }

    public AtomicDouble(String initStrVal) {
        this(Double.valueOf(initStrVal));
    }

    // Atomic methods
    public Double getDoubleValue() {
        return value.get();
    }
```

```
public void set(double newVal) {
    value.set(new Double(newVal));
}

public void lazySet(double newVal) {
    set(newVal);
}

public boolean compareAndSet(double expect, double update) {
    Double origVal, newVal;

    newVal = new Double(update);
    while (true) {
        origVal = getDoubleValue();

        if (Double.compare(origVal.doubleValue(), expect) == 0) {
            if (value.compareAndSet(origVal, newVal))
                return true;
        } else {
            return false;
        }
    }
}

public boolean weakCompareAndSet(double expect, double update) {
    return compareAndSet(expect, update);
}

public double getAndSet(double setVal) {
    while (true) {
        double origVal = get();

        if (compareAndSet(origVal, setVal)) return origVal;
    }
}

public double getAndAdd(double delta) {
    while (true) {
        double origVal = get();
        double newVal = origVal + delta;
        if (compareAndSet(origVal, newVal)) return origVal;
    }
}

public double addAndGet(double delta) {
    while (true) {
        double origVal = get();
        double newVal = origVal + delta;
        if (compareAndSet(origVal, newVal)) return newVal;
```

```java
        }
    }

    public double getAndIncrement() {
        return getAndAdd((double) 1.0);
    }

    public double getAndDecrement() {
        return getAndAdd((double) -1.0);
    }

    public double incrementAndGet() {
        return addAndGet((double) 1.0);
    }

    public double decrementAndGet() {
        return addAndGet((double) -1.0);
    }

    public double getAndMultiply(double multiple) {
        while (true) {
            double origVal = get();
            double newVal = origVal * multiple;
            if (compareAndSet(origVal, newVal)) return origVal;
        }
    }

    public double multiplyAndGet(double multiple) {
        while (true) {
            double origVal = get();
            double newVal = origVal * multiple;
            if (compareAndSet(origVal, newVal)) return newVal;
        }
    }

    // Methods of the Number class
    @Override
    public int intValue() {
        return getDoubleValue().intValue();
    }

    @Override
    public long longValue() {
        return getDoubleValue().longValue();
    }

    @Override
    public float floatValue() {
        return getDoubleValue().floatValue();
```

```
    }

    @Override
    public double doubleValue() {
        return getDoubleValue().doubleValue();
    }

    @Override
    public byte byteValue() {
        return (byte)intValue();
    }

    @Override
    public short shortValue() {
        return (short)intValue();
    }

    public char charValue() {
        return (char)intValue();
    }

    public boolean isNaN() {
        return getDoubleValue().isNaN();
    }

    public boolean isInfinite() {
        return getDoubleValue().isInfinite();
    }

    // Support methods for hashing and comparing
    @Override
    public String toString() {
        return getDoubleValue().toString();
    }

    @Override
    public boolean equals(Object obj) {
        if (obj == null) return false;
        if (obj instanceof Double) return (compareTo((Double)obj) == 0);
        if (obj instanceof AtomicDouble)
                return (compareTo((AtomicDouble)obj) == 0);
        return false;
    }

    @Override
    public int hashCode() {
        return getDoubleValue().hashCode();
    }
```

```
    public int compareTo(Double aValue) {
        return comparator.compare(this, aValue);
    }

    public int compareTo(AtomicDouble aValue) {
        return comparator.compare(this, aValue);
    }

    public static AtomicDoubleComparator comparator =
                                    new AtomicDoubleComparator();
    public final static class AtomicDoubleComparator
                    implements Comparator<AtomicDouble> {
        public int compare(AtomicDouble d1, AtomicDouble d2) {
            return Double.compare(d1.doubleValue(), d2.doubleValue());
        }

        public int compare(Double d1, AtomicDouble d2) {
            return Double.compare(d1.doubleValue(), d2.doubleValue());
        }

        public int compare(AtomicDouble d1, Double d2) {
            return Double.compare(d1.doubleValue(), d2.doubleValue());
        }
    }
}
```

AtomicDouble class

Now that we have an AtomicDouble class, let's see what happens if we replace synchronization with a global AtomicDouble.

```
public class PiAtomic
{
    private static final int NUM_THREADS = 8;
    private static final double step = 0.125 * (1.0 / (4.0 * 1024.0 *
1024.0)); //will use 2^25 steps to calculate pi
    private static AtomicDouble pi = new AtomicDouble(0);
    public static void main(String[] args)
    {
        long start = System.currentTimeMillis();
        int i = 0;
        IntegrationThread[] threads = new IntegrationThread[NUM_THREADS];
        while (i < NUM_THREADS)
        {
            threads[i] = new IntegrationThread(i * 0.125, (i+1) * 0.125);
//integrate from start to end
            threads[i].start();
            i++;
        }

        i = 0;
        while (i < NUM_THREADS)
        {
            while (true)
            {
                try
                {
                    threads[i].join();
                    break;
                }
                catch(InterruptedException e)
                {
                    continue;
                }
            }
            i++;
        }

        System.out.println("Pi is approximately " + pi);
        long end = System.currentTimeMillis();
        System.out.println("Execution took " + (end-start) + "ms");
    }

    private static final class IntegrationThread extends Thread
    {
        private double start;
        private double end;

        public IntegrationThread(double start, double end)
        {
```

```
                this.start = start;
                this.end = end;
        }

        public void run()
        {
            while (start < end)
            {
                double temp = ((16.0 * start - 16.0) / (Math.pow(start, 4)
 - 2 * Math.pow(start, 3) + 4 * start - 4)) * step;
                pi.getAndAdd(temp);
                start += step;
            }
        }
    }
}
```

Using a global AtomicDouble

If you were expecting this version to perform better, you will be disappointed. This version takes 12295ms to complete on the same machine. That's 7% worse! That's the first key point. The atomic classes offerred by Java are extremely powerful and can often be used to improve performance of variables that need synchronization. But, it is not always the right thing to use. In this case, there is so much contention on the global variable that all the compare-and-swap operations actually take longer than just acquiring a monitor and updating the variable. The atomic classes are still very useful and you should read the Java documentation on them if you are not familiar enough with them.

The last change we will make illustrates the other key point. Always do as much of the calculation as possible locally in each thread. This minimizes the contention on shared data. Sometimes, this is best achieved by using a local thread variable. Sometimes, it makes sense to use ThreadLocal objects. Sometimes, you really need a custom version of ThreadLocal that you write yourself. If you are not familiar with ThreadLocal, now would be a good time to go read the Java documentation for it. In the next chapter, you will see an example of a time where we need a custom ThreadLocal.

```java
public class PiLocal
{
    private static final int NUM_THREADS = 8;
    private static final double step = 0.125 * (1.0 / (4.0 * 1024.0 *
1024.0)); //will use 2^25 steps to calculate pi
    private static AtomicDouble pi = new AtomicDouble(0);
    public static void main(String[] args)
    {
        long start = System.currentTimeMillis();
        int i = 0;
        IntegrationThread[] threads = new IntegrationThread[NUM_THREADS];
        while (i < NUM_THREADS)
        {
            threads[i] = new IntegrationThread(i * 0.125, (i+1) * 0.125);
//integrate from start to end
            threads[i].start();
            i++;
        }

        i = 0;
        while (i < NUM_THREADS)
        {
            while (true)
            {
                try
                {
                    threads[i].join();
                    break;
                }
                catch(InterruptedException e)
                {
                    continue;
                }
            }
            i++;
        }

        System.out.println("Pi is approximately " + pi);
        long end = System.currentTimeMillis();
        System.out.println("Execution took " + (end-start) + "ms");
    }

    private static final class IntegrationThread extends Thread
    {
        private double start;
        private double end;

        public IntegrationThread(double start, double end)
        {
```

```
            this.start = start;
            this.end = end;
        }

        public void run()
        {
            double temp = 0;
            while (start < end)
            {
                temp += ((16.0 * start - 16.0) / (Math.pow(start, 4) - 2 *
Math.pow(start, 3) + 4 * start - 4)) * step;
                start += step;
            }
            pi.getAndAdd(temp);
        }
    }
}
```

Performing as much computation locally in the thread

This version is obviously the most well-written, and it is no surprise that it comes in at 1721ms. That's a whopping 85% improvement over the original version.

ReentrantLock and ReentrantReadWriteLock

It's hard to come up with contrived examples for ReentrantLock and ReentrantReadWriteLock. So, instead I'll just explain their usage. Hopefully, my explanation will give you an idea of where you may be able to take advantage of these in your applications. ReentrantLock can sometimes help performance a little bit, and ReentrantReadWriteLock can often help performance considerably.

ReentrantLock can be used as a replacement for synchronization. When you need the lock, you call the lock() method of ReentrantLock. To free the lock you call unlock(). The main difference is that you can release the lock inside of a block, whereas synchronization always ends when the end of the block is reached. This means that you may be able to release the lock earlier than you could have with synchronization. This can potentially mean increased concurrency.

ReentrantReadWriteLock is different. Imagine you have 2 methods a() and b(). Method a() cannot run if b() is running, and b() cannot run if a() is running. This is a classic example of the need for synchronization. But further assume that a() can be called and executed by multiple threads simultaneously without the need for synchronization. If you use synchronization, only 1 thread can execute a() at a time. A ReentrantReadWriteLock internally has 2 locks, a read lock and a write lock. There is no limit to the number of threads that can lock the read lock concurrently. But, a write lock can only be obtained when there are no read locks, and a read lock cannot be obtained when a write lock is held.

By using the read lock to lock method a(), in our example, and the write lock to lock method b(), we can achieve these goals. Multiple threads can concurrently run a(), but we can guarantee that b() is never running if any a()'s are running

ConcurrentSkipListMap and ConcurrentHashMap

I will end this chapter with a quick comment about 2 very important classes for good multi-threaded code. If you need thread-safe tree maps or hash maps, do not use Collections.synchronizedMap(). You should instead use ConcurrentHashMap for hash maps and ConcurrentSkipListMap for tree maps. If you do not know what a skip list is, I suggest you look it up. Wikipedia has a great explanation of skip lists. But rest assured, it is a map and will order your data just like a tree map. Both of these classes have excellent performance and excellent concurrency.

5 IMPROVING CODE EFFICIENCY

In this chapter, we will look at the remaining things you can do to improve performance. Some of these things you will have heard before and will think are common knowledge. But, I try to present these items with benchmark comparisons that actually illustrate how big the difference can be. There's a lot of material here that covers a wide range of different types of optimization. Hopefully, you will find that several of these are applicable to your applications.

StringBuilder

I'm sure you've heard it over and over again. Alays use StringBuilder to build strings instead of using +. However, many people tend to assume that the performance impact is small and that the ease of using + outweighs the small performance improvement. I'm here to tell you that the performance improvement is not small at all. Let's look at a simple example that shows a common usage of the + operator.

```java
import java.util.Random;

public class NoStringBuilder
{
    public static void main(String[] args)
    {
        long start = System.currentTimeMillis();
        Random random = new Random();
        int i = 0;
        while (i < 1000)
        {
            String string = Integer.toString(random.nextInt());
            int j = 1;
            while (j < 1000)
            {
                string += ("," + random.nextInt());
                j++;
            }

            //System.out.println(string);
            i++;
        }

        long end = System.currentTimeMillis();
        System.out.println("Execution took " + (end-start) + "ms");
    }
}
```

Building strings with the + operator

I also built a program that does the same thing but uses StringBuilder instead.

```java
import java.util.Random;

public class WithStringBuilder
{
    public static void main(String[] args)
    {
        long start = System.currentTimeMillis();
        Random random = new Random();
        int i = 0;
        while (i < 1000)
        {
            StringBuilder string = new StringBuilder();
            string.append(Integer.toString(random.nextInt()));
            int j = 1;
            while (j < 1000)
            {
                string.append("," + random.nextInt());
                j++;
            }

            //System.out.println(string.toString());
            string.toString();
            i++;
        }

        long end = System.currentTimeMillis();
        System.out.println("Execution took " + (end-start) + "ms");
    }
}
```

Building strings with StringBuilder

On my machine, the execution time of the version that uses the + operator is 17501ms. The version that uses StringBuilder is 983ms. Yes, you read that correctly! That's a 94% performance improvement. Obviously, I am creating strings of a 1000 items, and the difference wouldn't be quite so great for shorter strings. But, this does illustrate that using StringBuilder can provide major performance improvements.

Custom Parsing

Java has lots of built-in functions that make it easy to parse data. Unfortunately, many of them have a bunch of options, support all kinds of data formats, and have lots of error checking. This means that they are much slower than they could be. If you know that the format of your data is always consistent, and you know that your data is valid, you can write custom parsing methods to parse your data much faster than the Java built-in functions. In this section, we will look at parsing numbers, dates, and tokens.

First let's look at a replacement for Long.parseLong(). This replacement method assumes that the data is always valid. The same ideas can be applied to a parseInt() replacement. First the example that uses the java built-in functions.

```java
import java.util.Random;

public class BuiltInParseLong
{
    private static final int NUM_ITER = 10000000;

    public static void main(String[] args)
    {
        long start = System.currentTimeMillis();
        Random random = new Random();
        int i = 0;
        while (i < NUM_ITER)
        {
            Long.parseLong(Integer.toString(random.nextInt()));
            i++;
        }
        long end = System.currentTimeMillis();
        System.out.println("Execution took " + (end-start) + "ms");
    }
}
```

Parsing ten million values with Long.parseLong()

Here is the version with our custom parsing routine.

```java
import java.util.Random;

public class CustomParseLong
{
    private static final int NUM_ITER = 10000000;

    public static void main(String[] args)
    {
        long start = System.currentTimeMillis();
        Random random = new Random();
        int i = 0;
        while (i < NUM_ITER)
        {
            parseLong(Integer.toString(random.nextInt()));
            i++;
        }
        long end = System.currentTimeMillis();
        System.out.println("Execution took " + (end-start) + "ms");
    }

    public static final long parseLong(String s)
```

```
    {
        boolean negative = false;
        int offset = 0;
        long result = 0;
        int length = s.length();

        if (s.charAt(0) == '-')
        {
            negative = true;
            offset = 1;
        }

        while (offset < length)
        {
            byte b = (byte)s.charAt(offset);
            b -= 48;
            result *= 10;
            result += b;
            offset++;
        }

        if (negative)
        {
            result *= -1;
        }

        return result;
    }
}
```

Parsing ten million values with a custom parse routine

As you can see, the custom parse routine is very simple. It just checks for a negative sign and then picks up each character, converts to an integer value via subtraction, and adds it to the result, shifting the previous result left one place. The performance difference is astonishing. On my machine, using the built-in parseLong() method made the program run for 3096ms. The version that used our custom parse method only took 2515ms. That's a 19% performance improvement.

We can do the same sort of thing for parseDouble() or parseFloat as well. It's a little trickier because of the fractional part, but not much. The basic idea is to ignore the decimal point and treat the integer and fractional parts as if they were all digits of an integer value. We then use our existing custom parseLong() method to parse that integer value. We then divide the result by the appropriate factor of 10 to get the correct floating-point value. First, I'll show an example like above that uses the built-in parseDouble(). Then I'll show an example that uses the custom parseDouble(). The custom parseDouble() will again assume that all data is valid. It also assumes that all data is in the format of xxxx.yyyy, i.e. no scientific notation. It will also accept integer values without a decimal point.

```
import java.util.Random;

public class BuiltInParseDouble
{
    private static final int NUM_ITER = 10000000;

    public static void main(String[] args)
    {
        long start = System.currentTimeMillis();
        Random random = new Random();
        int i = 0;
        while (i < NUM_ITER)
        {
            Double.parseDouble(random.nextInt() + "." +
random.nextInt(Integer.MAX_VALUE));
            i++;
        }
        long end = System.currentTimeMillis();
        System.out.println("Execution took " + (end-start) + "ms");
    }
}
```

Parsing ten million doubles with the built-in parseDouble()

The example that uses the built-in parseDouble() method took 71341ms! That shows how much slower it is than parseLong(). Now, here is the example using the custom method.

```
import java.util.Random;

public class CustomParseDouble
{
    private static final int NUM_ITER = 10000000;

    public static void main(String[] args)
    {
        long start = System.currentTimeMillis();
        Random random = new Random();
        int i = 0;
        while (i < NUM_ITER)
        {
            parseDouble(random.nextInt() + "." +
random.nextInt(Integer.MAX_VALUE));
            i++;
        }
        long end = System.currentTimeMillis();
        System.out.println("Execution took " + (end-start) + "ms");
    }
```

```
public static final long parseLong(String s)
{
    boolean negative = false;
    int offset = 0;
    long result = 0;
    int length = s.length();

    if (s.charAt(0) == '-')
    {
        negative = true;
        offset = 1;
    }

    while (offset < length)
    {
        byte b = (byte)s.charAt(offset);
        b -= 48;
        result *= 10;
        result += b;
        offset++;
    }

    if (negative)
    {
        result *= -1;
    }

    return result;
}

public static final double parseDouble(String s)
{
    int p = s.indexOf('.');
    if (p < 0)
    {
        return parseLong(s);
    }

    boolean negative = false;
    int offset = 0;
    if (s.charAt(0) == '-')
    {
        negative = true;
        offset = 1;
    }

    while (s.charAt(offset) == '0')
    {
        offset++;
```

```
        }

        String s2 = s.substring(offset, p) + s.substring(p+1, s.length());
        long n = parseLong(s2);
        int x = s.length() - p - 1;
        int i = 0;
        long d = 1;
        while (i < x)
        {
            d *= 10;
            i++;
        }

        double retval = (n*1.0) / (d*1.0);
        if (negative)
        {
            retval *= -1;
        }

        return retval;
    }
}
```

Parsing ten million doubles with a custom parse method

Using the custom parseDouble() method brings the elapsed time down to 25019ms, a 65% improvement. That's huge!

For those of you who have worked with Dates (yes I know everything about them is deprecated, but they are still so easy and usefull), you know how painfully slow it is to use SimpleDateFormat to parse Dates. Next, we will show a custom Date class and a custom method for parsing dates. First, here's the version using java.util.Date and SimpleDateFormat. We will assume that dates are always in the format of yyyy-mm-dd (or yyyy-MM-dd for those familiar with format string syntax).

```java
import java.text.ParseException;
import java.text.SimpleDateFormat;
import java.util.Random;

public class BuiltInParseDate
{
    private static final int NUM_ITER = 10000000;
    private static final SimpleDateFormat sdf = new
SimpleDateFormat("yyyy-MM-dd");

    public static void main(String[] args)
    {
        long start = System.currentTimeMillis();
        Random random = new Random();
        int i = 0;
        while (i < NUM_ITER)
        {
            try
            {
                sdf.parse((random.nextInt(11) + 2004) + "-" +
(random.nextInt(12) + 1) + "-" + (random.nextInt(28) + 1));
            }
            catch(ParseException e)
            {
                e.printStackTrace();
                System.exit(1);
            }
            i++;
        }
        long end = System.currentTimeMillis();
        System.out.println("Execution took " + (end-start) + "ms");
    }
}
```

Parsing ten million dates with SimpleDateFormat

This version used a whopping 88808ms! There is a lot of stuff going on in Date and SimpleDateFormat that you typically don't need. Let's build a stripped down version that just parses and stores dates in this specific format. Notice that the custom date parser relies on a custom parseInt() that is modeled after the custom parseLong() that we created earlier.

```
import java.text.ParseException;
import java.text.SimpleDateFormat;
import java.util.Random;

public class CustomParseDate
{
    private static final int NUM_ITER = 10000000;
    private static final MySimpleDateFormat sdf = new
MySimpleDateFormat("yyyy-MM-dd");

    public static void main(String[] args)
    {
        long start = System.currentTimeMillis();
        Random random = new Random();
        int i = 0;
        while (i < NUM_ITER)
        {
            sdf.parse((random.nextInt(11) + 2004) + "-" +
(random.nextInt(12) + 1) + "-" + (random.nextInt(28) + 1));
            i++;
        }
        long end = System.currentTimeMillis();
        System.out.println("Execution took " + (end-start) + "ms");
    }

    public static final int parseInt(String s)
    {
        boolean negative = false;
        int offset = 0;
        int result = 0;
        int length = s.length();

        if (s.charAt(0) == '-')
        {
            negative = true;
            offset = 1;
        }

        while (offset < length)
        {
            byte b = (byte)s.charAt(offset);
            b -= 48;
            result *= 10;
            result += b;
            offset++;
        }

        if (negative)
        {
```

```
            result *= -1;
        }

        return result;
    }

    public static final class MySimpleDateFormat
    {
        public MySimpleDateFormat(String format)
        {}

        public static final MyDate parse(String s)
        {
            int firstIndex = s.indexOf('-');
            int secondIndex = s.indexOf('-', firstIndex+1);
            String year = s.substring(0, firstIndex);
            String month = s.substring(firstIndex+1, secondIndex);
            String day = s. substring(secondIndex+1);
            int iYear = parseInt(year);
            int iMonth = parseInt(month);
            int iDay = parseInt(day);
            return new MyDate(iYear, iMonth, iDay);
        }

        public String format(Object date)
        {
            MyDate d = (MyDate)date;
            return d.format();
        }
    }


    public static final class MyDate implements Comparable
    {
        protected int year;
        protected int month;
        protected int day;

        public MyDate(int year, int month, int day)
        {
            this.year = year;
            this.month = month;
            this.day = day;
        }

        public String format()
        {
            StringBuilder b = new StringBuilder();
            b.append(year);
```

```
            b.append("-");
            if (month < 10)
            {
                b.append("0");
            }
            b.append(month);
            b.append("-");
            if (day < 10)
            {
                b.append("0");
            }
            b.append(day);
            return b.toString();
        }

        public boolean equals(Object r)
        {
            MyDate rhs = (MyDate)r;
            return (year == rhs.year && month == rhs.month && day ==
rhs.day);
        }

        public int compareTo(Object r)
        {
            MyDate rhs = (MyDate)r;
            if (year < rhs.year)
            {
                return -1;
            }
            else if (year > rhs.year)
            {
                return 1;
            }
            else
            {
                if (month < rhs.month)
                {
                    return -1;
                }
                else if (month > rhs.month)
                {
                    return 1;
                }
                else
                {
                    if (day < rhs.day)
                    {
                        return -1;
                    }
```

```
                    else if (day > rhs.day)
                    {
                        return 1;

                    }
                    else
                    {
                        return 0;
                    }
                }
            }
        }

        public String toString()
        {
            return this.format();
        }
    }
}
```

Using custom Date and SimpleDateFormat classes

The custom version only took 17872ms, an 80% improvement! Hopefully this section has shown you that there is a lot of potential for performance improvement by writing your own parsing methods. Your specific requirements, and therefore the specifics of your parsing methods, may be different. But, this sort of idea can be applied to almost any situation.

Before we move on to a different topic, there is one last type of parsing that I frequently encounter, and that can be improved on. I frequently use StringTokenizer to parse delimited data (comma, pipe, etc). I never want the delimiters returned, and sometimes I need additional features such as the ability to get an array of all the tokens, or to position to a certain index within the set of tokens. This led me to create my own custom StringTokenizer, which can handle the additional functions I need plus outperform the built-in version. Let's look at an example of parsing comma – delimited lines of text.

```
import java.util.Random;
import java.util.StringTokenizer;

public class BuiltInStringTokenizer
{
    private static final int NUM_ITER = 10000000;
    private static final int NUM_FIELDS_PER_LINE = 10;

    public static void main(String[] args)
    {
        long start = System.currentTimeMillis();
        Random random = new Random();
        int i = 0;
        while (i < NUM_ITER)
        {
            int j = 1;
            StringBuilder sb = new StringBuilder();
            sb.append(random.nextInt());
            while (j < NUM_FIELDS_PER_LINE)
            {
                sb.append("," + random.nextInt());
                j++;
            }
            StringTokenizer tokens = new StringTokenizer(sb.toString(),
",", false);
            while (tokens.hasMoreTokens())
            {
                String string = tokens.nextToken();
            }
            i++;
        }
        long end = System.currentTimeMillis();
        System.out.println("Execution took " + (end-start) + "ms");
    }
}
```

Parsing ten million lines of delimited text with StringTokenizer

This version, using StringTokenizer wasn't very fast, using 113638ms. Let's look at the version that uses the custom StringTokenizer.

```java
import java.util.Random;
import java.util.StringTokenizer;

public class CustomStringTokenizer
{
    private static final int NUM_ITER = 10000000;
    private static final int NUM_FIELDS_PER_LINE = 10;

    public static void main(String[] args)
    {
        long start = System.currentTimeMillis();
        Random random = new Random();
        FastStringTokenizer tokens = new FastStringTokenizer("", ",",
false);
        int i = 0;
        while (i < NUM_ITER)
        {
            int j = 1;
            StringBuilder sb = new StringBuilder();
            sb.append(random.nextInt());
            while (j < NUM_FIELDS_PER_LINE)
            {
                sb.append("," + random.nextInt());
                j++;
            }
            tokens.reuse(sb.toString(), ",", false);
            while (tokens.hasMoreTokens())
            {
                String string = tokens.nextToken();
            }
            i++;
        }
        long end = System.currentTimeMillis();
        System.out.println("Execution took " + (end-start) + "ms");
    }

    public static final class FastStringTokenizer
    {
        protected String[] result;
        protected int index;
        protected String delim;
        protected String string;
        protected String[] temp;

        public final void reuse(String string, String delim, boolean bool)
        {
            this.delim = delim;
            this.string = string;
            char delimiter = delim.charAt(0);
```

```
            if (temp.length < string.length() / 2 + 1)
            {
                temp = new String[string.length() / 2 + 1];
            }

            int wordCount = 0;
            int i = 0;
            int j = string.indexOf(delimiter);

            while (j >= 0)
            {
                temp[wordCount++] = string.substring(i, j);
                i = j + 1;
                j = string.indexOf(delimiter, i);
            }

            if (i < string.length())
            {
                temp[wordCount++] = string.substring(i);
            }

            if (result.length != wordCount)
            {
                result = new String[wordCount];
            }

            System.arraycopy(temp, 0, result, 0, wordCount);
            index = 0;
    }

    public FastStringTokenizer(String string, String delim, boolean
bool)
    {
        this.delim = delim;
        this.string = string;
        char delimiter = delim.charAt(0);

        temp = new String[string.length() / 2 + 1];
        int wordCount = 0;
        int i = 0;
        int j = string.indexOf(delimiter);

        while (j >= 0)
        {
            temp[wordCount++] = string.substring(i, j);
            i = j + 1;
            j = string.indexOf(delimiter, i);
        }
```

```
        if (i < string.length())
        {
            temp[wordCount++] = string.substring(i);
        }

        result = new String[wordCount];
        System.arraycopy(temp, 0, result, 0, wordCount);
        index = 0;
    }

    public boolean hasMoreTokens()
    {
        return index < result.length;
    }

    public String nextToken()
    {
        return result[index++];
    }

    public String[] allTokens()
    {
        return result;
    }

    public void setIndex(int index)
    {
        this.index = index;
    }
}
}
```

Parsing ten million delimited lines with a custom tokenizer

The custom version took 94956ms. It's not a huge improvement, but it's still a 16% improvement. It would be huge in a program that had to parse billions of lines (such as some of mine). Notice that I take my own advice and have a reuse() method that allows the reuse of the FastStringTokenizer object instead of creating a new one each time.

ThreadPool

There are many different types of ThreadPools that Java offers. In this sections I will be focused on the most basic of types; the ones returned by Executors.*newCachedThreadPool()*. The main advantage of thread pools is that there is a lot of overhead in creating threads. Thread pools allow you to reuse existing threads for new tasks, thus avoiding the overhead. Threads that are unused for a period of time are destroyed so that memory usage remains contained.

Unfortunately, it is not the easiest thing to take an application that is written using Threads and change it to use thread pools. However, in this section I will show you a sneaky way that makes it so easy it is almost transparent. Step 1 is to allocate a singleton thread pool via Executors.*newCachedThreadPool()*. I typically choose to put this in the ResourceMonitor or ResourceManager class that I have in almost every application (see the previous 2 chapters). Second, change all your threads to extend ThreadPoolThread instead of Thread. The code for ThreadPoolThread is below. That's it assuming you only use start() and join(). If you use other Thread methods, they shouldn't be that hard to add to ThreadPoolThread.

```java
import java.util.concurrent.ExecutionException;
import java.util.concurrent.Future;

public abstract class ThreadPoolThread implements Runnable
{
    protected Future forJoin;

    public void start()
    {
        forJoin = ResourceManager.pool.submit(this);
    }

    public void join() throws InterruptedException
    {
        try
        {
            forJoin.get();
        }
        catch(ExecutionException e)
        {}
    }
}
```

ThreadPoolThread

This approach is so easy, it just amazes me that I haven't seen it documented anywhere! Most documentation goes into complicated, invasive means of doing the Thread->thread pool migration.

Custom Serialization

For those who have been around Java for a while, you know that Java serialization is horribly slow and takes up way too much space. If you need performance, it's a good rule of thumb to never use Java serialization. There are numerous ways you can do custom serialization of Java objects, and there are many articles available on the web that discuss alternatives. Since there is so much available material already out there (with benchmarks), I decided not to provide one here. However, here are some great references on the web on this topic:
- https://code.google.com/p/kryo/
- http://www.javacodegeeks.com/2010/07/java-best-practices-high-performance.html
- http://code.google.com/p/fast-serialization/
- http://mechanical-sympathy.blogspot.com/2012/07/native-cc-like-performance-for-java.html

- http://java.dzone.com/articles/fast-java-file-serialization
- http://java-performance.info/various-methods-of-binary-serialization-in-java/

Sending Messages With Queues

It is a common practice to use a BlockingQueue to send messages between threads in Java. We use BlockingQueues instead of unbounded queues to constrain the amount of memory that will be used. Most commonly ArrayBlockingQueue or LinkedBlockingQueue would be used, but it depends on your specific requirements. In this section, I will show you how you can use buffering to create a blocking queue that is capable of much higher throughput rates than either ArrayBlockingQueue or LinkedBlockingQueue.

Let's start off with a simple single producer, single consumer throughput test using ArrayBlockingQueue. Note that the fast version that we will build is capable of doing multi-producer, multi-consumer as well.

```java
import java.util.Random;
import java.util.concurrent.ArrayBlockingQueue;

public class ArrayBlockingQueueThroughputTest
{
    private static final int QUEUE_SIZE = 1000000;
    private static final int NUM_MESSAGES = 10000000;
    private static final ArrayBlockingQueue q = new
ArrayBlockingQueue(QUEUE_SIZE);

    public static void main(String[] args)
    {
        long start = System.currentTimeMillis();
        Producer producer = new Producer();
        producer.start();
        Consumer consumer = new Consumer();
        consumer.start();
        while (true)
        {
            try
            {
                producer.join();
                break;
            }
            catch(InterruptedException e)
            {
                continue;
            }
        }

        while (true)
        {
            try
```

```
                consumer.join();
                break;
            }
            catch(InterruptedException e)
            {
                continue;
            }
        }

        long end = System.currentTimeMillis();
        System.out.println("Throughput was " + (NUM_MESSAGES * 1.0 / (end-
start)) + "msg/ms");
    }

    public static final class Producer extends Thread
    {
        public void run()
        {
            int i = 0;
            Random random = new Random();
            while (i < NUM_MESSAGES)
            {
                while (true)
                {
                    try
                    {
                        q.put(random.nextInt());
                        break;
                    }
                    catch(InterruptedException e)
                    {
                        continue;
                    }
                }

                i++;
            }
        }
    }

    public static final class Consumer extends Thread
    {
        public void run()
        {
            int i = 0;
            while (i < NUM_MESSAGES)
            {
                while (true)
                {
```

```
                        try
                        {
                            int j = (Integer)q.take();
                            break;
                        }
                        catch(InterruptedException e)
                        {
                            continue;
                        }
                    }

                    i++;
                }
            }
        }
    }
```

Throughput test using ArrayBlockingQueue

Using ArrayBlockingQueue, I achieved a throughput of 527 messages per millisecond on my machine. Now, let's create the improved version. The idea is that put() and take() on the ArrayBlockingQueue are more expensive operations. We can reduce the number of times those are called if we send arrays of messages instead of one message at a time. To do this, we have an array buffer on the input and output sides. On the input side, we put new messages into the input array buffer until it is full. Then we write the whole buffer to the queue. On the target side, we remove the whole buffer from the queue and use it as an output buffer to feed messages back to the application. When the output buffer is empty another buffer will be fetched from the queue.

There are only 3 modifications needed to the code. First we have to use our custom BufferedArrayBlockingQueue class instead of ArrayBlockingQueue. Second we have to flush the queue when we are done writing to it, since it is bufferred. Third, we know longer have to handle the InterruptedExceptions ourselves, since they are handled internally by BufferedArrayBlockingQueue. Here is the new version of the application code.

```java
import java.util.Random;
import java.util.concurrent.ArrayBlockingQueue;

public class BufferedArrayBlockingQueueThroughputTest
{
    private static final int QUEUE_SIZE = 1000000;
    private static final int NUM_MESSAGES = 10000000;
    private static final BufferedArrayBlockingQueue q = new
BufferedArrayBlockingQueue(QUEUE_SIZE);

    public static void main(String[] args)
    {
        long start = System.currentTimeMillis();
        Producer producer = new Producer();
        producer.start();
        Consumer consumer = new Consumer();
        consumer.start();
        while (true)
        {
            try
            {
                producer.join();
                break;
            }
            catch(InterruptedException e)
            {
                continue;
            }
        }

        while (true)
        {
            try
            {
                consumer.join();
                break;
            }
            catch(InterruptedException e)
            {
                continue;
            }
        }

        long end = System.currentTimeMillis();
        System.out.println("Throughput was " + (NUM_MESSAGES * 1.0 / (end-
start)) + "msg/ms");
    }

    public static final class Producer extends Thread
```

```
    {
        public void run()
        {
            int i = 0;
            Random random = new Random();
            while (i < NUM_MESSAGES)
            {
                q.put(random.nextInt());
                i++;
            }

            q.flush();
        }
    }

    public static final class Consumer extends Thread
    {
        public void run()
        {
            int i = 0;
            while (i < NUM_MESSAGES)
            {
                int j = (Integer)q.take();
                i++;
            }
        }
    }
}
```

Throughput test using BufferedArrayBlockingQueue

Finally, here is the implementation of BufferedArrayBlockingQueue itself. You'll see that it cleverly uses a custom implementation of ThreadLocal to achieve high levels of concurrency for multiple producers or consumers.

```
import java.util.concurrent.ArrayBlockingQueue;
import java.util.concurrent.ConcurrentHashMap;
import java.util.concurrent.ArrayBlockingQueue;

public final class BufferedArrayBlockingQueue
{
    protected final static int BLOCK_SIZE = 256;
    protected ConcurrentHashMap<Thread, ArrayAndIndex> threadLocal = new
ConcurrentHashMap<Thread, ArrayAndIndex>();
    protected ConcurrentHashMap<Thread, ArrayAndIndex> receives = new
ConcurrentHashMap<Thread, ArrayAndIndex>();
    protected ArrayBlockingQueue q;

    public BufferedArrayBlockingQueue(int cap)
    {
        q = new ArrayBlockingQueue(cap / BLOCK_SIZE);
    }

    public void clear()
    {
        receives.clear();
        threadLocal.clear();
        q.clear();
    }

    public void flush()
    {
        for (ArrayAndIndex oa : threadLocal.values())
        {
            while (true)
            {
                try
                {
                    synchronized(oa)
                    {
                        if (oa.oa[0] != null)
                        {
                            q.put(oa.oa);
                            oa.oa = new Object[BLOCK_SIZE];
                            oa.index = 0;
                        }
                    }

                    break;
                }
                catch(InterruptedException e)
                {}
            }
        }
    }
```

```
    }

    public Object peek()
    {
        ArrayAndIndex oa = receives.get(Thread.currentThread());
        if (oa == null)
        {
            while (true)
            {
                try
                {
                    Object[] os = (Object[])q.poll();
                    if (os == null)
                    {
                        return null;
                    }
                    oa = new ArrayAndIndex(os);
                    receives.put(Thread.currentThread(), oa);
                    break;
                }
                catch(Exception e)
                {}
            }
        }

        return oa.peek(q);
    }

    public void put(Object o)
    {
        if (o == null)
        {
            System.out.println("Null object placed on queue");
            Thread.dumpStack();
            System.exit(1);
        }
        ArrayAndIndex oa = threadLocal.get(Thread.currentThread());
        if (oa == null)
        {
            oa = new ArrayAndIndex();
            threadLocal.put(Thread.currentThread(), oa);
        }

        oa.put(o, q, threadLocal);
    }

    public Object take()
    {
        ArrayAndIndex oa = receives.get(Thread.currentThread());
```

```
        if (oa == null)
        {
            while (true)
            {
                try
                {
                    Object[] os = (Object[])q.take();
                    //Object[] os = take2();
                    oa = new ArrayAndIndex(os);
                    receives.put(Thread.currentThread(), oa);
                    break;
                }
                catch(Exception e)
                {}
            }
        }

        return oa.take(q);
    }

    private final static class ArrayAndIndex
    {
        protected volatile Object[] oa;
        protected int index = 0;

        public ArrayAndIndex()
        {
            oa = new Object[BLOCK_SIZE];
        }

        public ArrayAndIndex(Object[] oa)
        {
            this.oa = oa;
        }

        private void put(Object o, ArrayBlockingQueue q,
ConcurrentHashMap<Thread, ArrayAndIndex> threadLocal)
        {
            synchronized(this.oa)
            {
                oa[index++] = o;
            }

            if (index == BLOCK_SIZE)
            {
                flush(q);
            }
        }
```

```
    private Object peek(ArrayBlockingQueue q)
    {
        if (index < BLOCK_SIZE && oa[index] != null)
        {
            return oa[index];
        }

        index = 0;
        oa[index] = null;
        while (oa[index] == null)
        {
            while (true)
            {
                try
                {
                    Object[] oas = (Object[])q.poll();
                    if (oas == null)
                    {
                        return null;
                    }
                    oa = oas;
                    break;
                }
                catch(Exception e)
                {}
            }
        }

        return oa[index++];
    }

    private Object take(ArrayBlockingQueue q)
    {
        if (index < BLOCK_SIZE && oa[index] != null)
        {
            return oa[index++];
        }

        index = 0;
        oa[index] = null;
        while (oa[index] == null)
        {
            while (true)
            {
                try
                {
                    oa = (Object[])q.take();
                    //oa = (Object[])take2();
                    break;
```

```
                }
                catch(Exception e)
                {}
            }
        }

        return oa[index++];
    }

    private void flush(ArrayBlockingQueue q)
    {
        while (true)
        {
            try
            {
                synchronized(this.oa)
                {
                    if (this.oa[0] != null)
                    {
                        q.put(this.oa);
                        this.oa = new Object[BLOCK_SIZE];
                        this.index = 0;
                    }
                }

                break;
            }
            catch(InterruptedException e)
            {}
        }
    }
}
}
```

Implementation of BufferedArrayBlockingQueue

The version using BufferedArrayBlockingQueue had a throughput of 5571 messages/ms on my machine. That more than a 10x improvement in throughput over the ArrayBlockingQueue version! This just reiterates the point that when you've done all the basic, obvious tuning, there are still major performance improvements to be had by using custom code instead of relying directly on Java built-in classes and methods.

GPU Offload

The final section of this book will discuss offloading code to GPUs from Java. GPUs can sometimes run a thousand threads in parallel and can be much faster than a CPU for easily parallelizable code. This section involves using JNI and writing some C code. It is by no means designed to teach you JNI or CUDA C programming. But, there is enough information here to get you started with writing your own GPU calls from Java.

First of all, I should point out that there are some projects out there designed to remove the need to write C CUDA code and JNI calls. The most promising one is Rootbeer: https://github.com/pcpratts/rootbeer1/. At the time of writing this book, Rootbeer is still in early stages and I was unable to get it to work for this example. But, it does look to have a lot of potential.

The scenario is that I had to parse and calculate a lot of prefix expressions which could include integer literals, floating-point literals, named variables, +, -, *, and /. Rather than doing them all sequentially on the CPU, I decided to batch them up into groups of approximately 32k and submit the group to the GPU for processing. The Java method that I call to submit the group to the GPU looks like this:

extendKernel(rows, prefixBytes, results, jobs.size(), first.poses.size(), first.master.size(), prefixBytes.length);

Rows is a 2 dimensional float array that has been flattened to 1 dimension. It contains the values of the named variables for each input row. PrefixBytes is a byte[] representation of the prefix notation expression that be applied to all input rows. Results is a float[] for the results to be stored in. Jobs.size() returns the number of input rows. First.poses.size() returns the number of named variables per row (all rows have the same number). First.master.size() returns the number of items in the prefix expression. Lastly, prefixBytes.length obviously returns the length of the prefixBytes byte[].

In my Java code this method is defined as:

private native void *extendKernel(***float[]** *rows,* **byte[]** *prefix,* **float[]** *results,* **int** *numJobs,* **int** *numCols,* **int** *numPrefixes,* **int** *prefixBytesLength);*

Next, I compiled my java code and used the javah command to generate a JNI header file containing the C definition of my extendKernel function.

javah –jni –cp <classpath> <fully qualified class name for class that has native method>

Next I started writing the native implementation of extendKernel() in a C code file named ExtendKernel.c. ExtendKernel.c is still running on a CPU. It does nothing more than convert from Java arrays to C pointers, call the GPU code, and clean up resources. Here's the code for ExtendKernel.c:

```
#include "org_exascale_testing_ExtendKernel.h"

void cudaExtend(float*, char*, float*, int, int, int, int);

JNIEXPORT void JNICALL Java_org_exascale_testing_ExtendKernel_extendKernel
  (JNIEnv * env, jobject thisPointer, jfloatArray rows, jbyteArray prefix,
jfloatArray results, jint numJobs, jint numCols, jint numPrefixes, jint
prefixBytesLength)
{
    //convert to float* rows
    float* nativeRows = (*env)->GetFloatArrayElements(env, rows, 0);
    //char* prefix
    char* nativePrefix = (*env)->GetByteArrayElements(env, prefix, 0);
    //float* results
    float* nativeResults = (*env)->GetFloatArrayElements(env, results, 0);

    cudaExtend(nativeRows, nativePrefix, nativeResults, numJobs, numCols,
numPrefixes, prefixBytesLength);

    (*env)->ReleaseFloatArrayElements(env, rows, nativeRows, 0);
    (*env)->ReleaseByteArrayElements(env, prefix, nativePrefix, 0);
    (*env)->ReleaseFloatArrayElements(env, results, nativeResults, 0);
}
```

ExtendKernel.c

ExtendKernel.c calls cudaExtend() to execute the GPU code. CudaExtend() is implemented in C, but is in another file call extend_kernel.cu. Files with a cu extension contain C plus CUDA code. CUDA is an API for running code on NVIDIA GPUs. They are compiled with the NVIDIA compiler (nvcc) instead of gcc.

The cudaExtend() function itself runs on the CPU and just copies the necessary data to the GPU, starts the GPU code, waits for completion of the GPU code, and copies the results back. The rest of extend_kernel.cu contains code that runs on the GPU. These are the functions marked with __global__ (the GPU entry point) and __device__ (subroutines that run on the GPU that are called from the __global__ function). The __global__ function is called the kernel.

First I'll show you the cuda_extend.cu code, and lastly we'll talk about how to compile, link, and load all of this stuff.

```
#include <string.h>
#include <stdlib.h>
#include <stdio.h>

#define gpuErrchk(ans) { gpuAssert((ans), __FILE__, __LINE__); }

extern "C"
{
__constant__ char parseStack[4096];

inline void gpuAssert(cudaError_t code, char *file, int line, bool
abort=true)
{
    if (code != cudaSuccess)
    {
        fprintf(stderr,"GPUassert: %s %s %d\n", cudaGetErrorString(code),
file, line);
        if (abort) exit(code);
    }
}

__device__ int myStrlen(char* string)
{
    char* temp = string;
    while (*temp != 0)
    {
        temp++;
    }

    return temp-string;
}

__device__ int parseLong(char* string)
{
    char* temp = string;
    int negative = 0;
    int offset = 0;
    long result = 0;
    int length = myStrlen(string);

    if (*temp == '-')
    {
        negative = 1;
        offset = 1;
    }

    while (offset < length)
    {
        char b = temp[offset];
```

```
            b -= 48;
            result *= 10;
            result += b;
            offset++;
    }

    if (negative != 0)
    {
        result *= -1;
    }

    return result;
}

__device__ float myStrtod(char* string)
{
    char newTemp[32];
    char* temp = string;
    int p = -1;
    while (*temp != 0 && p == -1)
    {
        if (*temp == '.')
        {
            p = temp - string;
        }

        temp++;
    }

    temp = string;
    if (p < 0)
    {
        return parseLong(string);
    }

    int negative = 0;
    int offset = 0;
    if (*temp == '-')
    {
        negative = 1;
        offset = 1;
    }

    while (temp[offset] == '0')
    {
        offset++;
    }

    int strlen = myStrlen(temp);
```

```
        int i = offset;
        int a = 0;
        while (i < p)
        {
            newTemp[a] = temp[i];
            i++;
            a++;
        }

        i++;
        while (i < strlen)
        {
            newTemp[a] = temp[i];
            i++;
            a++;
        }
        newTemp[a] = 0;
        temp = newTemp;
        long n = parseLong(temp);
        int x = strlen - p - 1;
        i = 0;
        long d = 1;
        while (i < x)
        {
            d *= 10;
            i++;
        }

        float retval = (n*1.0f) / (d*1.0f);
        if (negative != 0)
        {
            retval *= -1.0f;
        }

        return retval;
}

__global__ void doExtendKernel(float* deviceRows, float* deviceResults,
int numJobs, int numCols, int numPrefixes, int prefixBytesLength, float*
execStack)
{
    int idx = blockIdx.x * blockDim.x + threadIdx.x;
    if (idx < numJobs)
    {
        int parseStackPtr = 0;
        int parseStackProcessed = 0;
        int esp = 512 * idx;
        int rowsCntr = 0;
```

```
    while (parseStackProcessed < numPrefixes)
    {
        char* temp = parseStack + parseStackPtr;
        if (*temp == '*')
        {
            esp--;
            float lhs = execStack[esp];
            esp--;
            float rhs = execStack[esp];
            execStack[esp] = lhs * rhs;
            esp++;
            parseStackPtr += 2;
            parseStackProcessed += 1;
        }
        else if (*temp == '-')
        {
            esp--;
            float lhs = execStack[esp];
            esp--;
            float rhs = execStack[esp];
            execStack[esp] = lhs - rhs;
            esp++;
            parseStackPtr += 2;
            parseStackProcessed += 1;
        }
        else if (*temp == '+')
        {
            esp--;
            float lhs = execStack[esp];
            esp--;
            float rhs = execStack[esp];
            execStack[esp] = lhs + rhs;
            esp++;
            parseStackPtr += 2;
            parseStackProcessed += 1;
        }
        else if (*temp == '/')
        {
            esp--;
            float lhs = execStack[esp];
            esp--;
            float rhs = execStack[esp];
            execStack[esp] = lhs / rhs;
            esp++;
            parseStackPtr += 2;
            parseStackProcessed += 1;
        }
        else
```

```
            {
                if ((*temp >= 'a' && *temp <= 'z') || (*temp >= 'A' &&
*temp <= 'Z') || (*temp == '_'))
                {
                    execStack[esp] = deviceRows[rowsCntr + idx * numCols];
                    rowsCntr++;
                    esp++;
                    parseStackPtr += (1 + myStrlen(temp));
                    parseStackProcessed++;
                }
                else
                {
                    float d = myStrtod(temp);
                    execStack[esp] = d;
                    esp++;
                    parseStackPtr += (1 + myStrlen(temp));
                    parseStackProcessed++;
                }
            }
        }
    }

    esp--;
    deviceResults[idx] = execStack[esp];
    }
}

void cudaExtend(float* nativeRows, char* nativePrefix, float*
nativeResults, int numJobs, int numCols, int numPrefixes, int
prefixBytesLength)
{
    float* deviceResults;
    float* deviceRows;
    //cuda malloc deviceResults
    gpuErrchk(cudaMalloc((void**)&deviceResults, numJobs *
sizeof(float)));
    //gpuErrchk(cudaMemset((void*)deviceResults, 0xFE, numJobs *
sizeof(float)));
    //cuda memcpy prefix
    gpuErrchk(cudaMemcpyToSymbol(parseStack, nativePrefix,
prefixBytesLength));
    //cuda malloc rows
    gpuErrchk(cudaMalloc((void**)&deviceRows, sizeof(float) * numJobs *
numCols));
    //cuda memcpy rows
    gpuErrchk(cudaMemcpy(deviceRows, nativeRows, sizeof(float) * numJobs *
numCols, cudaMemcpyHostToDevice));
    float* execStack;
    gpuErrchk(cudaMalloc((void**)&execStack, sizeof(float) * 512 *
numJobs));
```

```
    //invoke kernel
    int blockSize = 128;
    int nBlocks = numJobs/blockSize + (numJobs%blockSize == 0?0:1);
    doExtendKernel <<< nBlocks, blockSize >>> (deviceRows, deviceResults,
numJobs, numCols, numPrefixes, prefixBytesLength, execStack);
    //copy deviceResults back to nativeResults
    gpuErrchk(cudaPeekAtLastError());
    gpuErrchk(cudaMemcpy(nativeResults, deviceResults, numJobs *
sizeof(float), cudaMemcpyDeviceToHost));
    gpuErrchk(cudaFree(deviceRows));
    gpuErrchk(cudaFree(deviceResults));
    gpuErrchk(cudaFree(execStack));
}
}
```

Extend_kernel.cu

To build the native code, you should first compile all of your .c files into .o files.

```
gcc -c *.c -O2 -shared -fPIC -I/usr/local/cuda/include -I/<PATH_TO_JAVA>/include -
I<PATH_TO_JAVA>/include/linux
```

Next compile all of your .cu files.

```
nvcc -c *.cu -I/usr/local/cuda/include -Xcompiler -fPIC
```

Lastly, we need to link all the object modules together into a shared library.

```
gcc -shared -fPIC -o libextend.so *.o -lrt -lm -lcudart -I/usr/local/cuda/include -
I/<PATH_TO_JAVA>/include -I/<PATH_TO_JAVA>/include/linux -L/usr/local/cuda/lib64
```

This creates a shared object library called libextend.so. You must specify –Djava.library.path=<DIRECTORY_CONTAINING_SO_LIBRARY> on the JVM command line options.

The only other step is that you need to load the shared object library at runtime in Java. The best way to do this is to add a static block to the class that is the main entry point to your program. In the static block, call System.loadLibrary() with the name of the library. This will cause Java to search in java.library.path for a file named lib<name>.so.

System.loadLibrary("extend");

That's all it takes to run code on a GPU from within a Java application. In my case, I saw around a 10% throughput improvement by making this change.

Index

ABOUT THE AUTHOR

Jason Arnold has been doing computer programming for 24 years. He holds a Bachelor's degree in Computer Science from Northern Illinois University, a Master's from DePaul University, and is a PhD candidate at Illinois Institute of Technology. His favorite languages are Java and assembly language. ☺ His primary area of interest is relational database internals.

www.ingramcontent.com/pod-product-compliance
Lightning Source LLC
LaVergne TN
LVHW080102070326
832902LV00014B/2381